The Coming Tests with Russia

Books by Walter Lippmann

A PREFACE TO POLITICS

DRIFT AND MASTERY

THE STAKES OF DIPLOMACY

THE POLITICAL SCENE

LIBERTY AND THE NEWS

PUBLIC OPINION

THE PHANTOM PUBLIC

MEN OF DESTINY

AMERICAN INQUISITORS

A PREFACE TO MORALS

INTERPRETATIONS 1931–1932

INTERPRETATIONS 1933–1935

THE METHOD OF FREEDOM

THE NEW IMPERATIVE

THE GOOD SOCIETY

U. S. FOREIGN POLICY: SHIELD OF THE REPUBLIC

U. S. WAR AIMS

THE COLD WAR: A STUDY IN U. S. FOREIGN POLICY

ISOLATION AND ALLIANCES:
    AN AMERICAN SPEAKS TO THE BRITISH

THE PUBLIC PHILOSOPHY

THE COMMUNIST WORLD AND OURS

THE COMING TESTS WITH RUSSIA

With William O. Scroggs

THE UNITED STATES IN WORLD AFFAIRS 1931

THE UNITED STATES IN WORLD AFFAIRS 1932

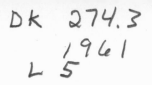

The Coming
Tests with Russia

by

WALTER LIPPMANN

An Atlantic Monthly Press Book
boston · Little, Brown and Company · toronto

LIBRARY OF CONGRESS CATALOG CARD NO. 61–14950

Second Printing

ATLANTIC–LITTLE, BROWN BOOKS
ARE PUBLISHED BY
LITTLE, BROWN AND COMPANY
IN ASSOCIATION WITH
THE ATLANTIC MONTHLY PRESS

*Published simultaneously in Canada
by Little, Brown & Company (Canada) Limited*

PRINTED IN THE UNITED STATES OF AMERICA

Editor's Note

MR. LIPPMANN had his first meeting with Mr. Khrushchev in the autumn of 1958, and at the conclusion he drew up a penetrating analysis of the Communist objectives as he had seen them emerge in their two-hour discussion. He emphasized that one of the fundamental differences between ourselves and the Russians is in our interpretation of "the *status quo*." "Whereas we think of the *status quo* as the situation as it exists at the moment, [Mr. Khrushchev] thinks of it as the process of revolutionary change which is in progress. He wants us to recognize the revolution not only as it is but as it is going to be." That is a hard truth which we must keep in mind as we prepare for the coming tests with Russia.

The second meeting of the two men took place

on April 10, 1961, at the Russian Premier's dacha at Sochi on the shores of the Black Sea. It was something of a family affair, beginning with a long private talk at 11:30 in the morning, at which Mr. Khrushchev, the official interpreter, and Mr. and Mrs. Lippmann were present, and running on for eight hours with time out for eating, drinking, and a game of badminton. (Mr. and Mrs. Lippmann played against Mr. Khrushchev and the woman interpreter.) Fateful events were impending, for this was on the eve of the launching of the Russian astronaut (of which Mr. Khrushchev said nothing); and the eve of the ill-judged invasion of Cuba, of which Mr. Khrushchev had been forewarned: he told Mr. Lippmann that it would be carried out by Cubans supplied with American arms, and that it would fail.

In the opening talk, which lasted until nearly three o'clock, and intermittently thereafter, Mr. Khrushchev opened his mind more freely and forcibly than he has to any other correspondent from the West. He spoke of disarmament, and dismissed the value for Russia of small nuclear weapons. He spoke of neutrality, and the inference to be drawn is that the Soviet Union will never again trust to "the neutrality" of an individual, such as Secretary General Hammarskjöld. ("You have not been troubled about this as long as you had the majority," Mr. Lippmann recalled his saying afterwards, "but when you lose the majority in the United Nations, as you will, the veto power will mean as much to you as it does to us.") The discussion ranged widely over the uncommitted nations, with Mr. Khrushchev specifying those which would be in a rebellious state, and quite confident that the revolution would succeed. But the most serious part of the confrontation centered in the discussion of the future of Germany, which Mr. Khrushchev clearly regards as the most sensitive issue between the East and the West. In realistic detail he looked ahead to the solution which he declares must be found in the near future.

This is an uncensored account of a vital and illuminating exchange. It was written down, the first part of it, on the plane flying the Lippmanns from Moscow to London and the balance in the English capital. It is a sobering blueprint of the designs of our greatest adversary which we will do well to keep in mind in the tense months ahead.

EDWARD WEEKS

Face to Face: I   3

Face to Face: II   13

Face to Face: III   21

Postscript: To Ourselves Be True   31

The Coming Tests with Russia

Face to Face: I

O N THIS, our second visit, my wife and I were taken on a long journey by plane and auto to Mr. Khrushchev's country place in Sochi on the Black Sea. Before we left Moscow, accompanied by two interpreters and an official of the Press Department, there was much mystery about all the details of the coming visit, such as when and where we were to see the great man. In fact, as it turned out, he had no other appointments after half past eleven in the morning, when he met us in the pine woods near the entrance of his place. Eight hours later, a bit worn by much talk and two large meals, we insisted on leaving in order to go to bed.

I would not like to leave the impression that all eight hours were devoted to great affairs of the world. Perhaps, all told, three and a half hours were spent in serious talk. The rest of the time went into the two prolonged meals at which Mr. Khrushchev, who is on what appears to be a nonfattening diet, broke the rules, saying joyously that the doctor had gone to Moscow for a day or two. The talk was largely banter between Mr. Khrushchev and Mikoyan (First Deputy Premier), who joined us for lunch, and the banter turned chiefly on Armenian food and Armenian wine and Armenian customs, which include the compulsion to drink all glasses to the end at each toast. Though we all drank a bit more than we wanted, Mikoyan chose to regard us as American ascetics who only sipped their wine. Finally Mr. Khrushchev took pity on us by providing a bowl into which we could pour the wine as fast as Mikoyan filled our glasses.

Between this heroic eating and drinking we walked around the place, which is large, met Mr. Khrushchev's grandson and Mikoyan's granddaughter, inspected the new and very gadgety swimming pool and, believe it or not, played badminton with Mr. Khrushchev.

In the serious talks, I might say that my wife made fairly full notes, I made a few jottings, but there was no transcript and the translation was done very ably by Mr. Victor M. Sukhodrev, who is an official in the Foreign Ministry. It was understood that I was free to write what I liked when I had left Russia and to quote Mr. Khrushchev or not to quote him as seemed desirable. I shall set down my own understanding and interpretation of the most important and interesting points that he made.

For an opening I reminded him that we had last seen him in October, 1958, nearly a year before his visit to the United States. Much has happened in these two and a half years and would he tell me what seemed to him the most important events for good or evil?

After a moment or two of hesitation, he replied that during this period the two main forces in the world — the Capitalist and the Socialist — have concluded that it was useless to "test" one another by military means. I took him to mean by "test" the backing of their political aims by the threat of war.

In contrast with 1958, when he professed to believe that the United States and Germany might attack him, he spoke with confidence that, because of the growing strength of the Communist orbit, the threat of war from our side was dying down. As a result, the United States was abandoning the "Dulles doctrine" that the neutrality of small states is "immoral." He himself welcomed President Kennedy's proposals for a neutral Laos.

You think then, I asked him, that there has been a change in United States policy? To this he replied that while there were some signs of a change, as for example in Laos, it was not a "radical" change, as could be seen in the United States attitude toward disarmament.

What, I asked him, is wrong with the United States attitude? We cannot see, he replied, that any change is imminent when the subject of disarmament is put in the hands of such a believer in armaments as Mr. McCloy. We think well of Mr. McCloy and during his time in Germany we had good relations with him. But asking him to deal with disarmament is a case of asking the goat to look after the cabbage patch.

I interjected the remark that the final decisions would be made by the President. But Mr. Khrushchev insisted that the forces behind the President would determine his policy. These forces behind the Kennedy administration he summed up in the one word "Rockefeller." The view that he is running the Kennedy administration will be news to Governor Rockefeller. I should add that Mr. Khrushchev considers me a Republican, which will be news to Mr. Nixon.

Then we got onto the subject of nuclear testing. He said that the Western powers were not ready to conclude an agreement, and that this was shown, among other things, by the demand for twenty-one or perhaps nineteen inspections a year.

He had been led personally to believe that the West would be satisfied with about three "symbolic" inspections. Nineteen inspections, our present demand, were nothing but a demand for the right to conduct complete reconnaissance of the Soviet Union.

I asked him about his attitude towards underground testing. He replied that the U. S. S. R. has never done any underground testing and never will.

I asked why? Because, he said, we do not see any value in small, tactical atomic weapons. If it comes to war, we shall use only the biggest weapons. The smaller ones are very expensive and they can decide nothing. The fact that they are expensive doesn't bother you because you don't care what you spend, and what is more many of your generals are connected with big business. But in the U. S. S. R. we have to economize, and tactical weapons are a waste. I report this without having the technical expertise to comment on it.

Then he went on to say that the second reason why he had no great hopes of an agreement was that the French are now testing and are unlikely to sign the agreement. It is obvious, he said, that if the French are not in the agreement, they will do the testing for the Americans. To which I said, and the Chinese will do the testing for you. He paused and then said that this was a fair remark. But, he added, while China is moving in the direction where she will be able to make tests, she is not yet able to make them. When the time comes that she can, there will be a new problem. We would like all states to sign a nuclear agreement.

Finally, he came to his third reason why an agreement may not be possible. It turns on the problem of the administrator of the agreement. Here, he was vehement and unqualified. He would never accept a single neutral administrator. Why? Because, he said, while there are neutral countries, there are no neutral men. You would not accept a Communist administrator and I cannot accept a non-Communist administrator. I will never entrust the security of the Soviet Union to any foreigner. We cannot have another Hammarskjold, no matter where he comes from among the neutral countries.

I found this enlightening. It was plain to me that here is a new dogma, that there are no neutral men. After all, the Soviet Union had accepted Trygve Lie and Hammarskjold. The Soviet Government has now come to the conclusion that there can be no such thing as an impartial civil servant in this deeply divided world, and that the kind of political celibacy which the British theory of the civil service calls for is in international affairs a fiction. This new dogma has long consequences. It means that there can be international co-operation only if, in the administration as well as in the policy-making, the Soviet Union has a veto.

Our talk went on to Cuba, Iran, revolutionary movements in general and finally to Germany. I shall report on these topics in subsequent articles.

Face to Face: II

IN THIS article I shall put together those parts of the talk which dealt with the revolutionary movements among small nations. Mr. Khrushchev spoke specifically of three of them — Laos, Cuba and Iran. But for him these three are merely examples of what he regards as a worldwide and historic revolutionary movement — akin to the change from feudalism to capitalism — which is surely destined to bring the old colonial countries into the Communist orbit. I could detect no doubt or reservation in his mind that this will surely happen, that there is no alternative, that while he will help this manifest destiny and while we will oppose it, the destiny would be realized no matter what either of us did.

Speaking of Iran, which he did without my raising the subject, he said that Iran had a very weak Communist party but that nevertheless the misery of the masses and the corruption of the government was surely producing a revolution. "You will assert," he said, "that the Shah has been overthrown by the Communists, and we shall be very glad to have it thought in the world that all the progressive people in Iran recognize that we are the leaders of the progress of mankind."

Judging by the general tenor of what he said about Iran, it would be fair to conclude that he is not contemplating military intervention and occupation — "Iran is a poor country which is of no use to the Soviet Union" — but that he will do all he can by propaganda and indirect intervention to bring down the Shah.

In his mind, Iran is the most immediate example of the inevitable movement of history in which he believes so completely. He would not admit that we can divert this historic movement by championing liberal democratic reforms. Nothing that any of us can say can change his mind, which is that of a true believer, except a demonstration in some country that we can promote deep democratic reforms.

His attitude towards Cuba is based on this same dogma. Castro's revolution is inevitable and predetermined. It was not made by the Soviet Union but by the history of Cuba, and the Soviet Union is involved because Castro appealed for economic help when the United States tried to strangle the revolution with an embargo.

He said flatly, but not, I thought, with much passion, that we were preparing a landing in Cuba, a landing not with American troops but with Cubans armed and supported by the United States. He said that if this happened, the Soviet Union would "oppose" the United States.

I hope I was not misled in understanding him to mean that he would oppose us by propaganda and diplomacy, and that he did not have in mind military intervention. I would in fact go a bit further, based not on what he said but on the general tone of his remarks, that in his book it is normal for a great power to undermine an unfriendly government within its own sphere of interest. He has been doing this himself in Laos and Iran and his feeling about the American support of subversion in Cuba is altogether different in quality from his feeling about the encouragement of resistance in the satellite states of Europe. Mr. Khrushchev thinks much more like Richelieu and Metternich than like Woodrow Wilson.

I had an over-all impression that his primary interest is not in the cold war about the small and underdeveloped countries. The support of the revolutionary movements among these countries is for him an interesting, hopeful, agreeable opportunity, but it is not a vital interest in the sense that he would go to war about it. He is quite sure that he will win this cold war without military force because he is on the side of history, and because he has the military power to deter us from a serious military intervention.

His primary concern is with the strong countries, especially with the United States, Germany, and China. I could not ask him direct questions about China. But there is no doubt that in his calculations of world power, China is a major factor. I felt that he thought of China as a problem of the future, and that may be one of the reasons why for him the immediate and passionate questions have to do with

[18]

Germany and disarmament. In my next article, I shall deal with what he had to say about Germany, which he discussed at some length.

For the present I should add a few miscellaneous impressions. During our walk after lunch, Mikoyan (First Deputy Premier) being with us then, I tried to find out what they thought of President Kennedy's purpose to bring the American economy not only out of the current recession but out of its chronic sluggishness. For quite evidently, much of his buoyant confidence in the historic destiny of the Soviet Union is based on the undoubted material progress of Soviet industry as compared with our slow rate of growth.

I had put the question to Mikoyan, assuming that he was the economic expert, but he deferred at once to Mr. Khrushchev. To Mr. Khrushchev it was certain that President Kennedy cannot succeed in accelerating American economic growth. He had, he told me, explained that to Mrs. Roosevelt when he was in New York during the American election. Why can't President Kennedy succeed? Because, he said, of "Rockefeller," and then added "Du Pont."

They will not let him. This was, it appears, one of those truths that cannot be doubted by any sane man.

None of this, however, was said with any personal animus against President Kennedy. Rather it was said as one might speak of the seasons and the tides and about mortality, about natural events which man does not control. While he has no confidence in the New Frontier, he has obvious respect for the President personally, though he confessed he could hardly understand how any man who had not been in a big government for a long time could suddenly become the head of it. Moreover, as I shall report tomorrow in talking about the German question, it is clear, I think, that he looks forward to another round of international negotiations before he precipitates a crisis over Berlin.

Face to Face: III

IT WAS clear to me at the end of a long talk that in Mr. Khrushchev's mind the future of Germany is the key question. I sought first to understand why he thinks the German problem is so urgent, and so I asked him whether, since agreement was so far off, a standstill of five or ten years might not be desirable. He said this was impossible. Why? Because there must be a German solution before "Hitler's generals with their twelve NATO divisions" get atomic weapons from France and the United States. Before this happens there must be a peace treaty defining the frontiers of Poland and Czechoslovakia and stabilizing the existence of the East German State. Otherwise, West Germany will drag NATO into a war for the unification of Germany and the restoration of the old eastern frontier.

His feeling of urgency, then, springs from two

[23]

causes: his need to consolidate the Communist East German state, the German Democratic Republic — known for short as the GDR — and second, his need to do this before West Germany is rearmed. He said several times that he would soon bring the German question to a head. Quite evidently, the possibility of nuclear arms for West Germany is not immediate. Bonn does not now have the weapons and although the possibility of it is real enough, the threat is not so urgent as to be a matter of a few months. The more immediately urgent consideration is, no doubt, the need to stabilize the East German regime, particularly in view of the flow of refugees.

My general impression was that he was firmly resolved, perhaps irretrievably committed, to a showdown on the German question. But it was evident also that he dreaded the tension — he referred to this several times — and is still looking for a negotiation which will work out a postponement and an accommodation.

In talks it transpired that he is thinking of the problem as having three phases.

The first is what he considers the real and also the eventual solution. He has no hope, however, that the West will now accept it. His thesis is as follows: The two Germanys cannot be reunited. The West will not agree to a unified Communist Germany and the Soviet Union will not agree to the absorption and destruction of the GDR by West Germany. There are in fact two Germanys. The way to proceed is, then, to "codify" the *status quo* in the form of peace treaties with what he called the three elements of Germany. These three elements are West Germany, East Germany, and West Berlin.

This codification would require *de facto* but not diplomatic recognition of the GDR. It would fix by international statute the position of West Berlin as "a free city," with its rights of access and its internal liberty guaranteed by the presence of "symbolic contingents" of French, British, American and Russian troops, by neutral troops under the aegis of the United Nations, and by the signatures of the two Germanys and the four occupying powers.

As I said above, Mr. Khrushchev does not expect

at this time to reach this solution. He has, there-fore, a second position which he called a "fallback" position. This is essentially that of the Soviets at the last Geneva conference of the foreign ministers. It would call for a temporary agreement. In the Russian view but not in our view this temporary agreement would have a short and fixed time limit of perhaps two to three years. During this time the two German states would be invited to negotiate on a form of unification — perhaps, though he did not say so specifically in this talk, a kind of loose con-federation. At the end of the fixed period of time, if a new agreement about West Berlin along the lines I have outlined previously was reached, it would be embodied in a treaty. If no agreement was reached, the legal rights of occupation would lapse.

This German solution was, as we know, refused by the West. But if there is to be another round of negotiation, variants on it are likely to be the sub-stance of the bargaining.

If this fails, Mr. Khrushchev's third position is that he will sign a separate peace treaty with East Germany. Then the GDR will in the Soviet view be sovereign over the rights of access to West Berlin. If the Western powers refuse to do business with the GDR and use force to enter West Berlin, then the Soviet government will use the Red Army to blockade West Berlin.

Though it would be foolish to undervalue his determination, the threat is not quite so fierce as it sounds. For he most certainly does not want a military showdown, and "doing business" with the GDR is a flexible and not a rigid conception.

I have confined myself strictly to reporting my understanding of the Soviet policy on Germany. If I may venture an opinion of my own, I would make these points.

First, Mr. Khrushchev will not precipitate a crisis until he has had a chance to talk face to face with President Kennedy.*

Second, he will surely sign a separate peace treaty if he cannot negotiate a temporary accommodation, which is described under his "second position."

* During the interview Mr. Khrushchev told me that there was the possibility of a meeting with the President early in June either in Vienna or Stockholm, and asked me to keep this news confidential except from the United States Ambassador.

Third, the crucial points which will determine whether the German question is resolved by negotiation or goes to a showdown are whether the prospect of nuclear arms for Germany increases or diminishes, and whether or not we say that the freedom of West Berlin, to which we are pledged, can be maintained only by a refusal to negotiate about this future.

I have been asked many times since we left the Soviet Union to come to London whether I found the whole interview encouraging or depressing. I found it sobering. On the one hand, the evidence was convincing that the U. S. S. R. is not contemplating war and is genuinely concerned to prevent any crisis, be it in Laos, in Cuba, or in Germany, from becoming uncontrollable. On the other hand, there is no doubt that the Soviet Government has a relentless determination to foster the revolutionary movement in the underdeveloped countries. This relentless determination springs from an unqualified faith in the predestined acceptance of Communism by the underdeveloped countries. The Soviet Government has great confidence in its own military forces. But it regards them not as an instrument of world conquest, but as the guardian against American interference with the predestined world revolution.

I was sobered by all this because I do not think there is any bluff in it.

To Ourselves Be True

WE HAVE been forced to ask ourselves recently how a free and open society can compete with a totalitarian state. This is a crucial question. Can our Western society survive and flourish if it remains true to its own faith and principles? Or must it abandon them in order to fight fire with fire?

There are those who believe that in Cuba the attempt to fight fire with fire would have succeeded if only the President had been more ruthless and had had no scruples about using American forces. I think they are wrong. I think that success for the Cuban adventure was impossible. In a free society like ours a policy is bound to fail which deliberately violates our pledges and our principles, our treaties and our laws. It is not possible for a free and open society to organize successfully a spectacular conspiracy.

The United States, like every other government, must employ secret agents. But the United States cannot successfully conduct large secret conspiracies. It is impossible to keep them secret. It is impossible for everybody concerned, beginning with the President himself, to be sufficiently ruthless and unscrupulous. The American conscience is a reality. It will make hesitant and ineffectual, even if it does not prevent, an un-American policy. The ultimate reason why the Cuban affair was incompetent is that it was out of character, like a cow that tried to fly or a fish that tried to walk.

It follows that in the great struggle with Communism, we must find our strength by developing and applying our own principles, not in abandoning them. Before anyone tells me that this is sissy, I should like to say why I believe it, especially after listening carefully and at some length to Mr. Khrushchev. I am very certain that we shall have the answer to Mr. Khrushchev if, but only if, we stop being fascinated by the cloak and dagger busi-

ness and, being true to ourselves, take our own principles seriously.

Mr. K. is a true believer that Communism is
destined to supplant capitalism as capitalism sup-
planted feudalism. For him this is an absolute
dogma, and he will tell you that while he intends to
do what he can to assist the inevitable, knowing
that we will do what we can to oppose the inevitable, what he does and what we do will not be
decisive. Destiny will be realized no matter what
men do.

The dogma of inevitability not only gives him the
self-assurance of a man who has no doubts but is a
most powerful ingredient of the Communist propaganda. What do we say to him, we who believe in a
certain freedom of the human will and in the ca-
pacity of men to affect the course of history by their
discoveries, their wisdom and their courage?

We can say that in Mr. K.'s dogma there is an
unexamined premise. It is that the capitalist society
is static, that it is and always will be what it was

[35]

when Marx described it a hundred years ago, that —
to use Mr. K.'s own lingo — there is no difference
between Governor Rockefeller and his grandfather.
Because a capitalist society cannot change, in its
dealings with the underdeveloped countries it can
only dominate and exploit. It cannot emancipate
and help. If it could emancipate and help, the inevitability of Communism would evaporate.

I venture to argue from this analysis that the reason we are on the defensive in so many places is that
for some ten years we have been doing exactly what
Mr. K. expects us to do. We have used money and
arms in a long losing attempt to stabilize native
governments which, in the name of anti-Commu-
nism, are opposed to all important social change.
This has been exactly what Mr. K.'s dogma calls for
— that Communism should be the only alternative
to the *status quo* with its immemorial poverty and
privilege.

We cannot compete with Communism in Asia,
Africa, or Latin America if we go on doing what
we have done so often and so widely — which is to
place the weak countries in a dilemma where they

[36]

must stand still with us and our client rulers or start moving with the Communists. This dilemma cannot be dissolved unless it is our central and persistent and unswerving policy to offer these unhappy countries a third option, which is economic development and social improvement without the totalitarian discipline of Communism.

For the only real alternative to Communism is a liberal and progressive society.

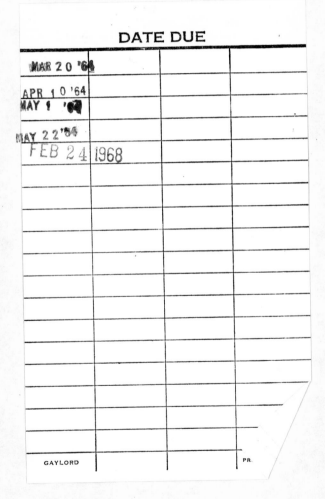

DATE DUE